AF430460

ISBN: 979-8-218-90261-2

Welcome

WE'RE SO GLAD
YOU'RE HERE

Parts of the Mass

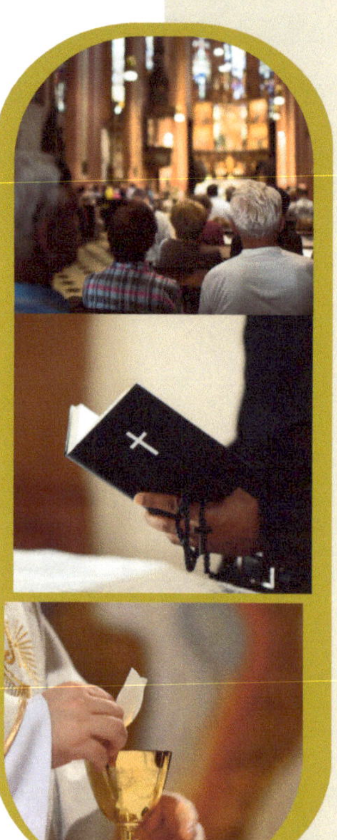

INTRODUCTORY RITES

Come, let us sing joyfully to the LORD.
Psalm 95:1

(Please stand for the processional hymn and procession.)

GREETING :

- In the name of the Father, and of the Son, and of the Holy Spirit.

R. Amen.

- *(Form A)* The grace of our Lord Jesus Christ, and the love of God, and the communion of the Holy Spirit be with you all.
- (Form B) Grace to you and peace from God our Father and the Lord Jesus Christ.
- (Form C) The Lord be with you.

R. And with your spirit.

INTRODUCTORY RITES

PENITENTIAL RITE :

- (Form A)

    I confess to almighty God / and to you, my brothers and sisters, / that I have greatly sinned, / in my thoughts and in my words, / in what I have done and in what I have failed to do, / (And, striking our breast 3x, we say:) through my fault, through my fault, / through my most grievous fault; / therefore I ask blessed Mary ever-Virgin, / all the Angels and Saints, / and you, my brothers and sisters, / to pray for me to the Lord our God.

- (Form B) Have mercy on us, O Lord.

    R. For we have sinned against you.

    Show us, O Lord, your mercy.

    R. And grant us your salvation.

- (Form C) You were sent to heal the contrite of heart: Lord, have mercy/Kyrie, eleison.

    R. Lord, have mercy/Kyrie, eleison.

    You came to call sinners: Christ, have mercy/Christe, eleison.

    R. Christ, have mercy/Christe, eleison.

    You are seated at the right hand of the Father to intercede for us: Lord, have mercy/Kyrie, eleison.

    R. Lord, have mercy/Kyrie, eleison.

    May almighty God have mercy on us, / forgive us our sins, / and bring us to everlasting life.

    R. Amen.

GLORIA :

(Omitted during Advent, Lent, and most weekdays.)

Glory to God in the highest, / and on earth peace to people of good will. / We praise you, / we bless you, / we adore you, / we glorify you, / we give you thanks for your great glory, / Lord God, heavenly King, / O God, almighty Father. / Lord Jesus Christ, Only Begotten Son, / Lord God, Lamb of God, Son of the Father, / you take away the sins of the world, / have mercy on us; / you take away the sins of the world, / receive our prayer; / you are seated at the right hand of the Father, / have mercy on us. / For you alone are the Holy One, / you alone are the Lord, / you alone are the Most High, / Jesus Christ, / with the Holy Spirit, / in the glory of God the Father. / Amen.

COLLECT :

Let us pray.

    R. Amen.

LITURGY OF THE WORD

And the Word became flesh and made his dwelling among us, and we saw his glory, the glory as of the Father's only Son, full of grace and truth.

John 1:16

FIRST READING :

(Please be seated.)

- The word of the Lord.
  R. Thanks be to God.

RESPONSORIAL PSALM :

(Repeat the response after the reader or cantor.)

SECOND READING :

(Only read on Sundays & certain liturgical days.)

- The word of the Lord.
  R. Thanks be to God.

GOSPEL :

(Please stand & repeat the Gospel Acclamation.)

- The Lord be with you.
  R. And with your spirit.
- A reading from the holy Gospel according to N.
  R. Glory to you, O Lord.

(During the response, make the sign on the cross with your thumb on your forehead, lips, and heart. You may say silently to yourself, "May the Word/Lord be in my thoughts, May the Word/Lord be in my words, May the Word/Lord be in my heart.)

- (After the Gospel reading.) The Gospel of the Lord.
  R. Praise to you, Lord Jesus Christ.

(Please be seated for the **HOMILY**.)

LITURGY OF THE WORD

PROFESSION OF FAITH - NICENE CREED:

(Please stand.)

I believe in one God,
the Father almighty,
maker of heaven and earth,
of all things visible and invisible.
I believe in one Lord Jesus Christ,
the Only Begotten Son of God,
born of the Father before all ages.
God from God, Light from Light,
true God from true God,
begotten, not made, consubstantial with the Father;
through him all things were made.
For us men and for our salvation
he came down from heaven, (bow your head)
and by the Holy Spirit was incarnate of the Virgin Mary,
and became man. (end bow)
For our sake he was crucified under Pontius Pilate,
he suffered death and was buried,
and rose again on the third day
in accordance with the Scriptures.
He ascended into heaven
and is seated at the right hand of the Father.
He will come again in glory
to judge the living and the dead
and his kingdom will have no end.
I believe in the Holy Spirit, the Lord, the giver of life,
who proceeds from the Father and the Son,
who with the Father and the Son is adored and glorified,
who has spoken through the prophets.
I believe in one, holy, catholic and apostolic Church.
I confess one Baptism for the forgiveness of sins
and I look forward to the resurrection of the dead
and the life of the world to come.
Amen.

UNIVERSAL PRAYER :

(Intentions are read aloud)

- We pray to the Lord.
    R. Lord, hear our prayer.

(Please be seated.)

LITURGY OF THE EUCHARIST

Whoever eats my flesh and drinks my blood has eternal life, and I will raise him on the last day. For my flesh is true food, and my blood is true drink. Whoever eats my flesh and drinks my blood remains in me and I in him.

John 6:54-56

OFFERTORY :

- Blessed are you, Lord God of all creation,
  for through your goodness we have received
  the bread we offer you:
  fruit of the earth and work of human hands,
  it will become for us the bread of life.
  R. Blessed be God for ever.
- Blessed are you, Lord God of all creation,
  for through your goodness we have received
  the wine we offer you:
  fruit of the vine and work of human hands,
  it will become our spiritual drink.
  R. Blessed be God for ever.

(Please stand.)

- Pray, brethren (brothers and sisters), / that my
  sacrifice and yours / may be acceptable to
  God, / the almighty Father.

*R. May the Lord accept the sacrifice at
your hands / for the praise and glory of
his name, / for our good / and the good
of all his holy Church.*

THE EUCHARISTIC PRAYER PREFACE :

- The Lord be with you.
  R. And with your spirit.

Lift up your hearts.
  R. We lift them up to the Lord.

Let us give thanks to the Lord our God.
  R. It is right and just.

LITURGY OF THE EUCHARIST

SANCTUS :

At the end of Priest's Preface, all sing or say:

Holy, Holy, Holy Lord God of hosts. / Heaven and earth are full of your glory. / Hosanna in the highest. / Blessed is he who comes in the name of the Lord. /
Hosanna in the highest.
OR
Sanctus, Sanctus, Sanctus Dominus Deus Sabaoth. / Pleni sunt caeli et terra gloria tua. / Hosanna in excelsis. / Benedictus qui venit in nomine Domini. /
Hosanna in excelsis.

(Please kneel for the Eucharistic Prayer.)

MEMORIAL ACCLAMATION :

- The mystery of faith.
  R. (Form A) *We proclaim your Death, O Lord, / and profess your Resurrection / until you come again.*

  (Form B) *When we eat this Bread and drink this Cup, / We proclaim your Death, O Lord, / until you come again.*

  (Form C) *Save us, Savior of the world, / for by your Cross and Resurrection / you have set us free.*

DOXOLOGY & AMEN :

- Through him, and with him, and in him, / O God, almighty Father, / in the unity of the Holy Spirit, / all glory and honor is yours, / for ever and ever.
  R. Amen.

THE LORD'S PRAYER :

(Please stand.)

- At the Savior's command and formed by divine teaching, we dare to say:
Our Father, who art in heaven, / hallowed be thy name; / thy kingdom come, / thy will be done / on earth as it is in heaven. / Give us this day our daily bread, / and forgive us our trespasses, / as we forgive those who trespass against us; / and lead us not into temptation, / but deliver us from evil.
- Deliver us, Lord, we pray, from every evil, / graciously grant peace in our days,/ that, by the help of your mercy, / we may be always free from sin / and safe from all distress, / as we await the blessed hope / and the coming of our Savior, Jesus Christ.
R. For the kingdom, the power and the glory are yours / now and for ever.
Amen.
- Lord Jesus Christ, / who said to your Apostles: / Peace I leave you, my peace I give you, / look not on our sins, / but on the faith of your Church, / and graciously grant her peace and unity / in accordance with your will. / Who live and reign for ever and ever.

R. Amen.

- The peace of the Lord be with you always.

R. And with your spirit.

- Let us offer each other the sign of peace.
(Offer those around you the sign of peace with a handshake, a simple wave of your hand, or a slight nod while saying *"Peace Be With You."*)

LAMB OF GOD / AGNUS DEI :

Lamb of God, you take away the sins of the world, have mercy on us. /
Lamb of God, you take away the sins of the world, have mercy on us. /
Lamb of God, you take away the sins of the world, grant us peace.
OR
Agnus Dei, qui tolis peccata mundi, miserere nobis. /
Agnus Dei, qui tolis peccata mundi, miserere nobis. /
Agnus Dei, qui tolis peccata mundi, dona nobis pacem.

(Please kneel.)

BEFORE COMMUNION :

- Behold the Lamb of God, / behold him who takes away the sins of the world. / Blessed are those called to the supper of the Lamb.

R. Lord, I am not worthy / that you should enter under my roof, / but only say the word / and my soul shall be healed.

COMMUNION :

- For Catholics: As Catholics, we fully participate in the celebration of the Eucharist when we receive Holy Communion. We are encouraged to receive Communion devoutly and frequently. In order to be properly disposed to receive Communion, participants should not be conscious of grave sin and normally should have fasted for one hour. A person who is conscious of grave sin is not to receive the Body and Blood of the Lord without prior sacramental confession except for a grave reason where there is no opportunity for confession. In this case, the person is to be mindful of the obligation to make an act of perfect contrition, including the intention of confessing as soon as possible (canon 916). A frequent reception of the Sacrament of Penance is encouraged for all.

- For our Fellow Christians: We welcome our fellow Christians to this celebration of the Eucharist as our brothers and sisters. We pray that our common baptism and the action of the Holy Spirit in this Eucharist will draw us closer to one another and begin to dispel the sad divisions which separate us. We pray that these will lessen and finally disappear, in keeping with Christ's prayer for us "that they may all be one" (Jn 17:21). Because Catholics believe that the celebration of the Eucharist is a sign of the reality of the oneness of faith, life, and worship, members of those churches with whom we are not yet fully united are ordinarily not admitted to Holy Communion. Eucharistic sharing in exceptional circumstances by other Christians requires permission according to the directives of the diocesan bishop and the provisions of canon law (canon 844 § 4). Members of the Orthodox Churches, the Assyrian Church of the East, and the Polish National Catholic Church are urged to respect the discipline of their own Churches. According to Roman Catholic discipline, the Code of Canon Law does not object to the reception of communion by Christians of these Churches (canon 844 § 3). 33

- For Those Not Receiving Communion: All who are not receiving Holy Communion are encouraged to express in their hearts a prayerful desire for unity with the Lord Jesus and with one another.

- For Non-Christians We also welcome to this celebration those who do not share our faith in Jesus Christ. While we cannot admit them to Holy Communion, we ask them to offer their prayers for the peace and the unity of the human family.

THE CONCLUDING RITES

He said to them, "Go into the whole world and proclaim the gospel to every creature.
Mark 16:15

BLESSING :

(Please stand.)

- The Lord be with you.
  R. And with your spirit.
- May almighty God bless you, the Father, and the Son, and the Holy Spirit. (make the sign of the cross)

  R. Amen.

DISMISSAL :

- (Form A) Go forth, the Mass is ended.
- (Form B) Go and announce the Gospel of the Lord.
- (Form C) Go in peace, glorifying the Lord by your life.

  R. Thanks be to God.
- (Form D- during the Octave of Easter & at Pentacost) Go In peace, alleluia, alleluia.

  R. Thanks be to God, alleluia, alleluia.

(Please remain standing for the recessional hymn.)

ST. MICHAEL PRAYER

Saint Michael the Archangel, defend us in battle; be our protection against the wickedness and snares of the devil. May God rebuke him, we humbly pray, and do thou, O Prince of the heavenly hosts, by the power of God, thrust into hell Satan and all the evil spirits who prowl about the world seeking the ruin of souls.
Amen

EGREDI!

Go, therefore, and make disciples of all nations, baptizing them in the name of
the Father, and of the Son, and of the holy Spirit
Matthew 28:19

If you have any questions regarding the Mass or Catholicism,
please contact your local Catholic parish and visit
www.usccb.org or another reputable Catholic resource.

We hope to see you again soon!

Until next time, may God bless
you and keep you.
Amen

HOW DO I BECOME CONFIRMED IN THE CATHOLIC FAITH?

And so I say to you, you are Peter, and upon this rock I will build my church, and the gates of the netherworld shall not prevail against it.
Matthew 16:18

WHAT IS OCIA? :

- Learning and reflection: Participants learn more about Catholic beliefs, practices, and traditions through instruction, study, and fellowship.
- Spiritual formation: To help individuals grow in their relationship with God and the Church community.
- Gradual conversion: The initiation process is organized into segments, with the time each person spends in each stage varying based on their individual journey.
- Sacraments of Initiation: For those who complete the OCIA process, the journey concludes with the celebration of the sacraments of Baptism (if applicable), Confirmation, and Holy Eucharist, typically at the Easter Vigil.

WHO IS OCIA FOR? :

- Unbaptized individuals: Those who have never been baptized and wish to become Catholic.
- Baptized Christians of other faiths: People who were baptized in another Christian denomination and want to enter full communion with the Catholic Church.
- Baptized Catholics: Baptized Catholics who have not yet received the sacraments of Confirmation and Holy Communion.
- Anyone seeking knowledge: People who are simply interested in learning more about the Catholic faith, even if they are not yet ready to fully commit to entering the Catholic Church.

NOTES

NOTES

NOTES

NOTES

QUESTIONS

QUESTIONS

QUESTIONS

QUESTIONS